PART I: FOUNDATIONS AND EVOLUTION

Origins of Cryptocurrencies: Beyond Bitcoin

Evolution of Consensus Models: Proof of Work, Proof of Stake, and Beyond

Comparative Analysis of First, Second and Third Generation Blockchains

Cryptocurrencies and Game Theory: Understanding Economic Incentives

Financial Democratization or New Elite? Sociological Analysis

PART II: IN-DEPTH ECONOMIC ASPECTS

Cryptocurrencies in Economic Crises: Refuge or Risk?

Analysis of Speculative Bubbles in the History of Cryptocurrencies

Cryptocurrencies and Tax Evasion: Issues and Solutions

Microeconomics of Non-Fungible Tokens (NFTs)

Cryptocurrencies and Wealth Redistribution

PART III: ENVIRONMENT AND SUSTAINABILITY

Blockchain and Circular Economy: Potential and Limits
Cryptocurrencies and Green Finance: Responsible Investments
Environmental Impact of Mining Farms
Development of Eco-responsible Blockchains
Cryptocurrencies and Natural Resource Management

PART IV: LITTLE-KNOWN INNOVATIONS AND APPLICATIONS

Blockchain in the Healthcare Sector: Confidentiality and Efficiency

Use of Cryptocurrencies in Conflict Zones and Humanitarian Crises

Blockchain and Governance: Electronic Voting and Beyond

Cryptocurrencies and Art: Beyond NFTs

Blockchain and Digital Identity Management

PART V: ARTIFICIAL INTELLIGENCE AND CRYPTOCURRENCIES

AI for Cryptocurrency Market Prediction
Self-Scaling Smart Contracts using AI
AI and Fraud Risk Analysis in Cryptocurrencies
Development of AI-Managed Cryptocurrencies
AI and Optimization of Blockchain Networks

PART VI: FUTURE PERSPECTIVES AND EXPLORATION

Cryptocurrencies in Space: Financing and Logistics of Space Missions

Blockchain and Internet of Things (IoT): Creating Autonomous Economies

Cryptocurrencies and the Quantum Economy: Preparing for the Future

Exploring Cryptocurrencies in Virtual Worlds and Metaverses

Prospective: Cryptocurrencies in 50 Years

This detailed plan aims to explore aspects often overlooked or little discussed in the study of cryptocurrencies, providing a richer and more diverse perspective on this ever-evolving field.

CHAPTER 1: ORIGINS OF CRYPTOCURRENCIES: BEYOND BITCOIN

Introduction

The world of cryptocurrencies is often synonymous with Bitcoin, the first and most famous digital currency. However, the history of cryptocurrencies is much richer and more complex, dating back decades before Bitcoin was created. This chapter aims to explore the origins of cryptocurrencies, highlighting the technological, economic and philosophical developments that paved the way for their emergence.

1. Cryptographic Precursors and Key Concepts
   - B-Money and Bit Gold: Before Bitcoin, ideas like Wei Dai's B-Money and Nick Szabo's Bit Gold introduced key concepts like proof of work and decentralization.
   - Hashcash and Proof of Work: Developed by Adam Back, Hashcash used proof of work to combat email spam, an idea that would become central to the creation of Bitcoin.

2. Socio-Economic Context
   - Cypherpunks and Libertarianism: The cypherpunk movement, advocating the use of cryptography to preserve privacy, has played a crucial role in the underlying philosophy of cryptocurrencies.
   - 2008 Financial Crisis: Distrust of traditional financial

institutions, exacerbated by the 2008 crisis, created fertile ground for the adoption of alternative currencies like Bitcoin.

3. Birth of Bitcoin and Its Impact
   - Satoshi Nakamoto's White Paper: Analysis of the Bitcoin white paper, published in 2008, which laid the theoretical and technical foundations of the first decentralized cryptocurrency.
   - Initial Reception and Adoption: How Bitcoin was received by the technology community and early adopters, and its rapid evolution as a cultural and economic phenomenon.

4. Beyond Bitcoin: Diversification and Evolution
   - Altcoins and Diversification: The emergence of altcoins (alternatives to Bitcoin) like Litecoin, Ripple, and Ethereum, each bringing innovations in speed, security, and functionality.
   - Smart Contracts and Ethereum: The introduction of smart contracts by Ethereum, marking a significant evolution in the possible applications of cryptocurrencies.

5. Lessons Learned and Legacy
   - Innovations and Failures: Analysis of the successes and failures in the early years of cryptocurrencies, and how they shaped the current landscape.
   - Legacy and Influence on Current Technologies: How ideas and technologies from early cryptocurrencies continue to influence the world of blockchain and beyond.

Conclusion

The origins of cryptocurrencies are deeply rooted in a history of seeking decentralization, security and financial autonomy. By understanding the developments that preceded Bitcoin, we can better appreciate the complexity and richness of the cryptocurrency ecosystem today. This chapter shed light not only on the technical aspects, but also on the socio-economic and philosophical motivations that led to the birth of these revolutionary digital currencies.

CHAPTER 2: EVOLUTION OF CONSENSUS MODELS: PROOF OF WORK, PROOF OF STAKE, AND BEYOND

Introduction

Consensus models are at the heart of how cryptocurrencies and blockchains work. They determine how transactions are validated and how the security and integrity of the network are maintained. This chapter explores the evolution of these models, from Proof of Work (PoW) to Proof of Stake (PoS) and beyond, highlighting their impacts and innovations.

1. Proof of Work (PoW): The Foundations
- Concept and Operation: Explanation of the PoW mechanism, where miners solve complex cryptographic problems to validate transactions and create new blocks.
- Bitcoin and PoW: How Bitcoin used PoW to create a decentralized and secure system, and the implications of this choice.
- Challenges and Criticisms: Analysis of challenges related to PoW, including high energy consumption and scale issues.

2. Proof of Stake (PoS): An Energy Efficient Alternative

- Principles of PoS: Overview of the PoS model, where the creation of blocks and validation of transactions depends on the participation of currency holders.
- Benefits of PoS over PoW: Reduced energy consumption, improved scale and security.
- Notable Implementations: Ethereum 2.0, Cardano, and other cryptocurrencies that have adopted or plan to adopt PoS.

3. Beyond PoW and PoS: Innovations and New Models
- Delegated Proof of Stake (DPoS): Explaining DPoS, a variation of PoS, where token holders vote for delegates to validate transactions.
- Proof of Authority (PoA) and Other Models: Exploration of alternative models like PoA, used in contexts where trust is centralized.
- Hybrid Consensus: Discussion of hybrid models that combine PoW and PoS to leverage the benefits of each system.

4. Implications for Security and Decentralization
- Blockchain Network Security: Analysis of how different consensus models affect security and attack resistance.
- Decentralization and Power Distribution: Assessment of the impact of each model on network decentralization and power distribution among participants.

5. Future of Consensus Models
- Future Trends and Innovations: Exploring current research into consensus models, including the integration of artificial intelligence and multi-chain systems.
- Impact on Cryptocurrency Adoption and Regulation: How evolving consensus models could influence widespread cryptocurrency adoption and regulatory approaches.

Conclusion

The evolution of consensus models is a crucial aspect of the evolution of cryptocurrencies and blockchain technology. By moving from PoW to PoS and other innovative models, the community seeks to solve problems such as energy consumption, security, and scalability. This chapter has highlighted not only the technical aspects of these models, but also their socio-economic and environmental implications, providing a comprehensive perspective on the future of blockchain technology.

CHAPTER 3: COMPARATIVE ANALYSIS OF FIRST, SECOND AND THIRD GENERATION BLOCKCHAINS

Introduction

The evolution of blockchain technology can be divided into three distinct generations, each bringing significant innovations and improvements. This chapter offers a comparative analysis of these generations, focusing on their characteristics, applications and impacts.

1. First Generation: The Birth of Blockchain
- Bitcoin and the Original Blockchain: Exploring Bitcoin as the first application of blockchain technology, focused on creating a decentralized digital currency.
- Features and Limitations: Analysis of key features such as PoW, security, and transparency, as well as limitations like scalability and energy consumption.

2. Second Generation: Introduction of Smart Contracts
- Ethereum and the Expansion of Features: Presentation of Ethereum as the pioneer of the second generation, introducing smart contracts and the possibility of creating

decentralized applications (DApps).
- Impact of Smart Contracts: Discussion of how smart contracts have expanded the uses of blockchain beyond financial transactions, including areas like gaming, decentralized finance (DeFi), and more.

3. Third Generation: Interoperability and Scalability
- Cardano, Polkadot, and Others: Introducing third-generation blockchains, which aim to address the scalability and interoperability issues faced by their predecessors.
- Key Innovations: Exploring technologies such as parallel blockchains, delegated proof of stake (DPoS), and layer 2 solutions.
- Interoperability and Sustainability: Analysis of the importance of interoperability for the future of blockchains and the emphasis placed on more sustainable and eco-responsible solutions.

4. Performance and Application Comparison
- Performance Analysis: Comparison of transaction speeds, costs, power consumption, and ease of use between different generations.
- Generation-Specific Applications: Discussion of how each generation has paved the way for unique and innovative applications across various industries.

5. Challenges and Future Prospects
- Current Challenges: Exploring the challenges each generation of blockchain faces, including issues of regulation, mainstream adoption, and security.
- Future of Blockchain: Thoughts on the future of blockchain technology, considering lessons learned from each generation and emerging trends.

Conclusion

First, second and third generation blockchains represent key milestones in the evolution of this revolutionary technology. Each generation has made significant improvements and innovations, paving the way for new applications and possibilities.

By understanding the strengths, weaknesses and unique contributions of each generation, one can better appreciate the future potential of blockchain and its impact on various sectors.

CHAPTER 4: CRYPTOCURRENCIES AND GAME THEORY: UNDERSTANDING ECONOMIC INCENTIVES

Introduction
Game theory, a branch of applied mathematics, plays a crucial role in understanding cryptocurrencies. It helps analyze the strategic behaviors of actors in an environment where interactions are essential. This chapter explores how game theory applies to cryptocurrencies, particularly in the design of economic incentives and securing networks.

1. Fundamentals of Game Theory in Cryptocurrencies
- Fundamentals: Introduction to key concepts in game theory, such as zero-sum games, dominant strategies, and the Nash equilibrium.
- Application to Cryptocurrencies: How these concepts apply to the dynamics of cryptocurrencies, particularly in the context of transaction validation and block creation.

2. Proof of Work and Game Theory
- Mining and Incentives: Analysis of how game theory explains miner behavior in the Proof of Work (PoW) model.

- Network Balance and Security: Discussion of how Nash equilibrium is achieved in PoW, ensuring network security and reliability.

3. Proof of Stake and Economic Incentives
   - Staking and Decision Making: Exploring the Proof of Stake (PoS) model through the lens of game theory, focusing on incentives for validators.
   - Risks and Rewards: How game theory helps balance risks and rewards in PoS, encouraging honest participation.

4. Gaming and Cryptocurrency Governance
   - Collective Decision Making: Application of game theory to cryptocurrency governance, analyzing how participants make collective decisions.
   - Voting Mechanisms and Incentives: Study of different voting mechanisms and their effectiveness in reflecting the interests of participants while avoiding manipulation.

5. Dilemmas and Challenges in Cryptocurrencies
   - Prisoner's Dilemma and Collaboration: Exploring situations where participants must choose between cooperation and competition, and how this affects network stability.
   - Incomplete Information Games: Discussion of the challenges posed by incomplete information games in the cryptocurrency ecosystem, such as speculation and market manipulation.

6. Future Prospects
   - Evolution of Consensus Models: Reflection on how game theory could influence the development of new consensus models.
   - Innovations and Regulation: Exploring the potential implications of game theory for future innovation in cryptocurrencies and their regulation.

Conclusion

Game theory provides a powerful framework for understanding and designing economic systems and incentives within the cryptocurrency ecosystem. By analyzing the strategic interactions between different actors, it helps ensure the security, stability and efficiency of these decentralized systems. This chapter highlighted the importance of game theory not only in understanding existing cryptocurrencies, but also in developing future technologies and policies.

ChatGPT can make mistakes. Consider checking important

CHAPTER 5: FINANCIAL DEMOCRATIZATION OR NEW ELITE? SOCIOLOGICAL ANALYSIS

Introduction
Cryptocurrencies have been hailed as tools for financial democratization, providing unprecedented access to financial systems. However, they have also been criticized for creating a new elite. This chapter offers a sociological analysis of this aspect, exploring the social and economic impacts of cryptocurrencies on different strata of society.

1. Promises of Democratization
- Expanded Access to Financial Services: Exploring how cryptocurrencies provide access to financial services in underbanked regions.
- Empowering Small Investors: Analysis of the impact of cryptocurrencies on small investors and their ability to participate in global financial markets.

2. Creation of a New Elite
- Wealth Concentration: Examining the concentration of wealth in the cryptocurrency space and the potential creation of a new financial elite.
- Technical and Educational Barriers: Discussion of barriers

to entry, such as technical complexity and the need for financial education, which may exclude certain groups.

3. Impact on Traditional Financial Systems
   - Challenge for Banks and Financial Institutions: Analysis of how cryptocurrencies challenge the business models of traditional banks.
   - Regulatory and Policy Responses: Exploring the responses of governments and regulators to the rise of cryptocurrencies.

4. Socio-Economic Inequalities
   - Geographic Distribution of Cryptocurrency Users: Study of the demographics of cryptocurrency users across the world and the resulting socio-economic inequalities.
   - Cryptocurrencies and Financial Inclusion: Evaluation of the effectiveness of cryptocurrencies in reducing poverty and improving financial inclusion.

5. Culture and Social Perception
   - Cryptocurrencies in Popular Culture: Analysis of the representation of cryptocurrencies in the media, popular culture and their impact on public perception.
   - Trust and Social Adoption: Exploring the factors that influence trust and adoption of cryptocurrencies by the general public.

6. Future Prospects
   - Potential for Social Change: Reflection on the potential of cryptocurrencies to bring about significant social change, particularly in the areas of equity and financial access.
   - Upcoming Challenges and Opportunities: Discussion of future challenges, such as the balance between innovation and regulation, and opportunities for fairer integration of cryptocurrencies.

Conclusion

Cryptocurrencies represent both a promise of financial democratization and the risk of creating a new elite. This chapter explored the nuances of this impact, highlighting the opportunities and challenges that cryptocurrencies present for different social groups. By understanding these dynamics, we can better understand the potential role of cryptocurrencies in shaping the future socio-economic structure.

CHAPTER 6: CRYPTOCURRENCIES IN ECONOMIC CRISES: REFUGE OR RISK?

Introduction

Cryptocurrencies, with their decentralized nature and their independence from traditional financial systems, have been perceived sometimes as refuges in times of economic crisis, sometimes as high-risk investments. This chapter examines the role of cryptocurrencies during periods of economic turbulence, assessing their reliability and performance as safe haven assets.

1. Cryptocurrencies as a Safe Haven
   - Stability in Times of Crisis: Analysis of when cryptocurrencies gained popularity as stable assets or safe havens during financial crises.
   - Comparison with Gold and Other Safe Haven Assets: Comparative study of cryptocurrencies with traditional safe haven assets like gold, in terms of performance and stability.

2. Risks and Volatility
   - Price Volatility: Examines the inherent volatility of cryptocurrencies and its impact on their reliability as an investment during crises.
   - Factors Contributing to Volatility: Analysis of factors that contribute to the volatility of cryptocurrencies, including speculation, regulations, and geopolitical events.

3. Cryptocurrencies and Financial Crises
- Reactions to Global Economic Crises: Case study on the performance of cryptocurrencies during specific economic crises, such as the 2008 financial crisis and the COVID-19 pandemic.
- Cryptocurrency Adoption in Times of Crisis: Exploring how economic crises influence the adoption and use of cryptocurrencies across the world.

4. Diversification and Risk Management
- Cryptocurrencies in Investment Portfolios: Discussion of the role of cryptocurrencies in investment portfolio diversification and risk management.
- Investment Strategies in Times of Crisis: Analysis of the strategies adopted by investors in cryptocurrencies during periods of economic crisis.

5. Regulations and Safety
- Impact of Regulations in Times of Crisis: Assessing the impact of regulatory changes on cryptocurrencies during economic crises.
- Security of Cryptocurrency Investments: Discussion of security measures and risks associated with investing in cryptocurrencies during periods of instability.

6. Future Prospects
- Cryptocurrencies in Future Crisis Scenarios: Reflections on the potential of cryptocurrencies as safe haven assets in future economic crises.
- Expected Developments and Innovations: Exploring innovations in the cryptocurrency space that could influence their role in times of crisis.

Conclusion

Cryptocurrencies present a complex profile as safe-haven assets during economic crises. They offer both unique opportunities for diversification and resilience, but also significant risks linked to their volatility and regulatory uncertainty. This chapter has highlighted the multiple facets of cryptocurrencies in the context of economic crises, providing a balanced perspective on their potential role as safe haven or risk assets.

CHAPTER 7: ANALYSIS OF SPECULATIVE BUBBLES IN THE HISTORY OF CRYPTOCURRENCIES

Introduction

The history of cryptocurrencies has been marked by several speculative bubbles, where rapid and often unsustainable price increases were followed by equally dramatic corrections. This chapter explores these speculative bubbles, examining their causes, consequences and lessons learned.

1. Nature of Speculative Bubbles
- Definition and Characteristics: Introduction to the concepts of speculative bubbles, with emphasis on their characteristics in the context of cryptocurrencies.
- Investor Psychology: Analysis of investor psychology and how it contributes to the formation and bursting of bubbles.

2. Historical Bubbles in Cryptocurrencies
- The Bitcoin Bubble of 2017: In-depth look at the Bitcoin bubble of 2017, including the factors that led to its rapid rise and subsequent fall.
- Other Significant Examples: Examining other speculative bubbles in cryptocurrency history, such as the early price surges of Ethereum and other altcoins.

3. Contributing Factors
- Speculation and Media Hype: Exploring the role of speculation and media attention in the creation of speculative bubbles.
- Influence of New Investors: Discussion of the impact of new investors attracted by quick wins, often without a deep understanding of the market.
- Role of Exchanges and ICOs: Analysis of how exchanges and initial coin offerings (ICOs) have contributed to certain bubbles.

4. Economic and Social Consequences
- Impact on Individual Investors: Assessing the impact of speculative bubbles on individual investors, particularly those who enter the market at the peak of the bubble.
- Effects on the Cryptocurrency Market: Discussion of how these bubbles have affected the overall perception of cryptocurrencies and their long-term adoption.

5. Regulation and Prevention
- Regulatory Responses: Examination of regulatory responses to speculative bubbles and their effectiveness in preventing future bubbles.
- Prevention Strategies for Investors: Advice and strategies for investors to avoid the pitfalls of speculative bubbles.

6. Lessons Learned and Future Perspectives
- Analysis of Past Trends: Thoughts on lessons learned from previous bubbles and how they can inform future investment strategies.
- Forecasts for the Future of Cryptocurrencies: Discussion of the future prospects of cryptocurrencies and the likelihood of new speculative bubbles.

Conclusion

Speculative bubbles in the history of cryptocurrencies offer important lessons about the volatile nature of these assets, investor psychology and the importance of balanced regulation. By understanding the causes and consequences of these events, investors and regulators can be better prepared to navigate the dynamic cryptocurrency market. This chapter has highlighted the importance of financial education and prudence in a field characterized by rapid innovation and volatility.

CHAPTER 8: CRYPTOCURRENCIES AND TAX EVASION: CHALLENGES AND SOLUTIONS

Introduction
Cryptocurrencies, with their decentralized nature and relative anonymity, have raised concerns about their potential use for tax evasion. This chapter explores the issues related to tax evasion via cryptocurrencies and examines the solutions proposed to remedy them.

1. Cryptocurrencies and Anonymity
   - Anonymous Nature of Transactions: Discussion of how the anonymity of cryptocurrency transactions can facilitate tax evasion.
   - Comparison with Traditional Financial Systems: Analysis of the differences between cryptocurrencies and traditional financial systems in terms of traceability and transparency.

2. Tax and Regulatory Issues
   - Challenges for Tax Authorities: Exploring the difficulties faced by tax authorities in tracking and taxing cryptocurrency transactions.
   - International Regulatory Frameworks: Examination of international efforts to integrate cryptocurrencies into

existing tax frameworks.

3. Tax Evasion Cases and Case Studies
- Notable Examples of Tax Evasion: Presentation of real cases where cryptocurrencies have been used for tax evasion.
- Analysis of Evasion Methods: Discussion of tactics and strategies used to avoid detection and taxation.

4. Technological and Regulatory Solutions
- Improving Transparency: Exploring technologies, such as public blockchains and transaction analysis tools, that can increase transparency.
- Regulations and Compliance: Discussion of the laws and regulations put in place to combat tax evasion via cryptocurrencies.

5. International Collaboration and Information Exchange
- Global Initiatives: Review of international initiatives for better collaboration and information exchange between countries.
- Balancing Privacy and Tax Compliance: Discussion on how to balance user privacy with tax compliance requirements.

6. Education and Awareness
- Role of Financial Education: Importance of financial education to educate cryptocurrency users about tax obligations.
- Tax Authority Awareness Campaigns: Presentation of the efforts of tax authorities to inform the public about the taxation of cryptocurrencies.

7. Future Prospects
- Evolution of Regulations: Thoughts on the future evolution of tax regulations regarding cryptocurrencies.
- Emerging Technologies and Taxation: Discussion on the potential impact of new blockchain technologies on the management of tax evasion.

Conclusion

Tax evasion via cryptocurrencies represents a complex challenge requiring a coordinated response involving technology, regulation and education. This chapter has highlighted key issues and potential solutions, emphasizing the importance of a balanced approach that protects both the integrity of tax systems and the privacy of users. By proactively addressing these issues, it is possible to ensure that cryptocurrencies are used responsibly and in compliance with tax laws.

CHAPTER 9: MICROECONOMICS OF NON-FUNGIBLE TOKENS (NFTS)

Introduction

Non-Fungible Tokens (NFTs) have revolutionized the concept of digital property, creating a new market and new economic dynamics. This chapter explores the microeconomics of NFTs, examining their creation, their value, and their impact on various sectors.

1. Understanding NFTs
- Definition and Characteristics: Introduction to NFTs, explaining what makes them unique compared to traditional digital assets.
- Blockchain Technology and NFTs: Discussion of how blockchain technology underpins NFTs and ensures their uniqueness and traceability.

2. Creation and Issue of NFTs
- Creation Process: Exploring the process of creating (or "minting") NFTs, including technical and creative aspects.
- Factors Determining Value: Analysis of factors that influence the value of NFTs, such as rarity, artist, history and community.

3. NFT Markets and Platforms
- NFT Market Dynamics: Examines the unique characteristics of the NFT market, including liquidity, volatility and trends.

- NFT Trading Platforms: Overview of the main NFT trading platforms and their role in facilitating transactions.

4. Use and Applications of NFTs
   - NFTs in Art and Culture: Discussion of the use of NFTs in the art world, including auctions and digital ownership.
   - NFTs in Video Games and Entertainment: Exploring the use of NFTs in video games and entertainment, and their impact on these industries.

5. Speculation and Investment in NFTs
   - NFTs as Investments: Analysis of the popularity of NFTs as investment assets and the associated risks.
   - Speculative Bubbles and Market Stability: Discussion of speculative bubbles in the NFT market and their potential long-term impact.

6. Ethical and Legal Issues
   - Copyright and Intellectual Property: Examining copyright and intellectual property issues related to NFTs.
   - Ethical and Environmental Considerations: Discussion of ethical and environmental concerns, including the ecological impact of mining NFTs.

7. Future Prospects
   - Upcoming Innovations and Developments: Thoughts on future innovations in the NFT space and their potential for integration into various sectors.
   - Long-Term Impact on the Digital Economy: Exploring the potential impact of NFTs on the global digital economy and traditional business models.

Conclusion

NFTs represent a significant advancement in the way digital property is perceived and managed, providing new opportunities and challenges. This chapter has shed light on the complexity of the microeconomics of NFTs, highlighting their disruptive potential as well as the ethical and practical questions they raise. As they continue to evolve, NFTs could redefine many aspects of digital interaction and value creation in the digital economy.

CHAPTER 10: CRYPTOCURRENCIES AND WEALTH REDISTRIBUTION

Introduction

Cryptocurrencies have been presented as potential instruments for wealth redistribution, capable of disrupting traditional financial structures. This chapter explores the impact of cryptocurrencies on the distribution of wealth globally, examining both the opportunities and challenges they present.

1. Potential for Redistribution by Cryptocurrencies
- Expanded Access to Financial Markets: Discussion of how cryptocurrencies provide broader access to financial markets, particularly for unbanked populations.
- Democratization of Investments: Analysis of how cryptocurrencies enable broader participation in investment opportunities.

2. Realities of Wealth Distribution in Cryptocurrencies
- Concentration of Wealth: Examining the current concentration of wealth in the cryptocurrency space and its implications.
- Volatility and Investment Risks: Discussion of the volatility of cryptocurrencies and its impact on investors of different wealth levels.

3. Cryptocurrencies in Developing Economies
- Impact on Emerging Economies: Exploring the impact

of cryptocurrencies on developing economies, including benefits and risks.
- Successful Use Cases: Showcasing examples where cryptocurrencies have helped improve financial access and redistribute wealth in emerging economies.

4. Barriers to Equitable Redistribution
- Technical Complexity and Financial Education: Analysis of technical barriers and the need for financial education that can limit access to cryptocurrencies.
- Government Regulations and Policies: Discussion of the role of government regulations and policies in facilitating or hindering the redistribution of wealth through cryptocurrencies.

5. Cryptocurrencies and Social Inequalities
- Cryptocurrencies and Wealth Inequality: Assessing the impact of cryptocurrencies on existing wealth inequalities.
- Ethical and Social Challenges: Exploring the ethical and social challenges posed by the growing adoption of cryptocurrencies.

6. Future Perspectives and Potential for Change
- Future Innovations and Developments: Thoughts on future innovations in the cryptocurrency space and their potential to foster a more equitable redistribution of wealth.
- Strategies for a More Equitable Distribution: Discussion of potential strategies for using cryptocurrencies as tools for wealth redistribution.

Conclusion

Cryptocurrencies present both opportunities and challenges for wealth redistribution. They offer significant potential to democratize access to financial markets and to positively influence developing economies. However, challenges such as wealth concentration, volatility and technical barriers must be addressed to fully realize this potential. This chapter highlights the importance of a balanced and informed approach to harnessing cryptocurrencies as tools for economic and social change.

NICOLASMAJEUR

2 / 2

CHAPTER 11: BLOCKCHAIN AND CIRCULAR ECONOMY: POTENTIAL AND LIMITS

Introduction

The integration of blockchain technology into the circular economy has considerable potential to improve traceability, transparency and resource efficiency. This chapter explores how blockchain can facilitate the transition to a more circular economy, while examining its limitations and challenges.

1. Principles of the Circular Economy
   - Definition and Objectives: Introduction to the key concepts of the circular economy, focused on reducing waste and maximizing the use of resources.
   - Current Challenges: Discussion on current challenges in implementing the circular economy, particularly in terms of traceability and resource management.

2. Role of Blockchain in the Circular Economy
   - Enhanced Traceability: Exploring how blockchain can provide unparalleled traceability of products and materials throughout their lifecycle.
   - Data Transparency and Reliability: Analysis of blockchain's ability to provide transparent and reliable data, essential for

an efficient circular economy.
3. Use Cases and Applications
- Waste Management and Recycling: Presentation of blockchain use cases to improve waste management and recycling processes.
- Sustainable Supply Chains: Examples of how blockchain is being used to create more sustainable and responsible supply chains.
4. Potential for Innovation and Collaboration
- Collaborative Platforms: Discussion on the potential of blockchain-based platforms to facilitate collaboration between different actors in the circular economy.
- Innovation in Business Models: Exploration of new business opportunities and economic models made possible by the integration of blockchain.
5. Limits and Challenges of Blockchain
- Energy Consumption: Examining the energy consumption of certain blockchains and its impact on sustainability goals.
- Technical Complexity and Adoption: Analysis of the challenges related to the technical complexity of blockchain and the obstacles to its widespread adoption.
6. Future Prospects
- Technological Developments: Reflections on future developments in blockchain technology that could improve its application in the circular economy.
- Integration with Other Technologies: Discussion on how blockchain could be integrated with other innovative technologies to strengthen the circular economy.

Conclusion

Blockchain offers exciting possibilities for advancing the circular economy, thanks to its ability to provide traceability, transparency and efficiency. However, to fully realize its potential, it is essential to overcome challenges related to energy consumption and technical complexity. This chapter highlights the potential role of blockchain as an enabler of the circular economy, while recognizing the limitations and challenges to successful integration.

CHAPTER 12: CRYPTOCURRENCIES AND GREEN FINANCE: RESPONSIBLE INVESTMENTS

Introduction

The intersection of cryptocurrencies and green finance represents an emerging and promising area. This chapter explores how cryptocurrencies can contribute to more responsible and sustainable investments, while examining the challenges and opportunities associated with this convergence.

1. Green Finance: Foundations and Importance
   - Principles of Green Finance: Introduction to key green finance concepts, including sustainability, responsible investment and environmental impact.
   - Role in the Fight against Climate Change: Discussion on the importance of green finance in the fight against climate change and the promotion of sustainable development.

2. Cryptocurrencies and Sustainability
   - Environmental Impact of Cryptocurrencies: Analysis of the environmental impact of cryptocurrencies, particularly with regard to mining energy consumption.
   - Greener Cryptocurrency Initiatives: Overview of efforts to make cryptocurrencies greener, including Proof of Work

alternatives and carbon offset projects.
3. Cryptocurrencies in Sustainable Investments
- Tokenization of Green Assets: Exploring the tokenization of green assets and its potential to democratize access to sustainable investments.
- Blockchain-Based Green Finance Projects and Platforms: Presentation of specific projects and platforms that use blockchain to facilitate green investments.

4. Transparency and Traceability
- Benefits of Blockchain for Green Finance: Discussion on how blockchain can improve transparency and traceability in green investments.
- Certification and Reporting of Sustainable Projects: Analysis of the use of blockchain for the certification and reporting of sustainable projects.

5. Challenges and Criticisms
- Integration Challenges: Examines the challenges of integrating cryptocurrencies into green finance, including regulatory and market issues.
- Ethical Criticisms and Concerns: Discussion of criticisms regarding the use of cryptocurrencies in green finance, particularly in terms of ethics and actual sustainability.

6. Future Outlook and Growth Potential
- Future Innovations in Green Finance and Cryptocurrencies: Thoughts on future innovations and growth potential of the intersection between green finance and cryptocurrencies.
- Potential Role in the Ecological Transition: Exploring the potential role of cryptocurrencies in facilitating the transition to a greener and sustainable economy.

Conclusion

Cryptocurrencies, despite their challenges, offer unique opportunities to promote responsible investments and support green finance. By improving transparency, traceability and access to sustainable investments, they can play a significant role in the transition to more sustainable financial practices. This chapter highlights the importance of overcoming current environmental and regulatory challenges to fully realize the potential of cryptocurrencies in promoting greener and responsible finance.

CHAPTER 13: ENVIRONMENTAL IMPACT OF MINING FARMS

Introduction
Cryptocurrency mining, particularly for currencies like Bitcoin, requires a significant amount of energy, raising environmental concerns. This chapter examines the environmental impact of cryptocurrency mining farms and explores potential solutions to reduce their ecological footprint.

1. Mining Process and Energy Consumption
- How Mining Farms Work: Explanation of the mining process, including the role of mining farms in validating transactions and creating new units of currency.
- High Energy Consumption: Analysis of the energy consumption of large mining farms and its impact on the environment.

2. Environmental Impact
- Greenhouse Gas Emissions: Assessment of CO_2 and other greenhouse gas emissions resulting from the intense activity of mining farms.
- Energy Resource Use: Discussion of energy sources used by mining farms, including renewable and non-renewable energy.

3. Geography of Mining Farms

- Global Distribution of Mining Farms: Examination of the geographic distribution of mining farms and their environmental impact in different regions.
- Mining Farm Migration: Analysis of mining farm relocation trends to regions offering cheaper or greener electricity.

4. Solutions and Innovations
- Greener Mining: Introducing initiatives to make cryptocurrency mining greener, including the use of renewable energy.
- Technological Innovations: Exploring technological advances, such as more efficient cooling systems and energy-efficient mining hardware.

5. Alternatives to Traditional Mining
- Alternative Consensus Models: Discussion of alternatives to the Proof of Work model, such as Proof of Stake, and their potentially reduced impact on the environment.
- Decentralization and Energy: Analysis of the relationship between the decentralization of cryptocurrencies and energy requirements.

6. Regulations and Policies
- Policy and Regulatory Responses: Review of government policies and regulations aimed at limiting the environmental impact of mining farms.
- Incentives for Sustainable Practices: Discussion of economic and fiscal incentives to encourage more sustainable mining practices.

7. Future Prospects
- Changing Mining Landscape: Thoughts on the future of cryptocurrency mining and its environmental impact.
- Role of Communities and Investors: Exploring the role that cryptocurrency communities and investors can play in promoting environmentally friendly mining practices.

Conclusion

The environmental impact of mining farms is a major concern in the world of cryptocurrencies. As demand for cryptocurrencies continues to grow, it is crucial to find ways to reduce their ecological footprint. This chapter highlights the need for a balanced approach that considers both the economic benefits of cryptocurrency mining and the compelling need to protect our environment.

CHAPTER 14: DEVELOPMENT OF ECO-RESPONSIBLE BLOCKCHAINS

Introduction
Faced with growing concerns about the environmental impact of blockchain technologies, particularly with regard to energy consumption, the development of eco-responsible blockchains has become a topic of primary importance. This chapter explores strategies and innovations to make blockchain more sustainable and environmentally friendly.

1. Environmental Issues of Current Blockchains
- Energy Consumption of Blockchains: Analysis of the high energy consumption associated with certain blockchain models, in particular those using the Proof of Work system.
- Carbon Impact: Assessment of the carbon footprint of blockchains and its impact on climate change.

2. Innovations in Ecological Consensus
- Proof of Stake: Introducing proof of stake as an energy efficient alternative to proof of work.
- Other Consensus Models: Exploring other innovative and less energy-intensive consensus models, such as Proof of Authority and Delegated Proof of Stake.

3. Use of Renewable Energy
- Blockchain and Green Energy: Discussion on the use of renewable energy to power blockchain infrastructures.

- Projects and Initiatives: Presentation of specific blockchain projects that use or encourage the use of renewable energy.

4. Optimization of Energy Efficiency
    - Technological Improvements: Exploring technological advances aimed at improving the energy efficiency of blockchains, including in mining hardware.
    - Reduction of Computational Load: Analysis of methods to reduce the computational load necessary for the operation of blockchains.

5. Regulations and Ecological Standards
    - Regulatory Frameworks: Examination of policies and regulations that could encourage or require the development of eco-responsible blockchains.
    - Standards and Certifications: Discussion on establishing standards and certifications to promote sustainable practices in the blockchain industry.

6. Awareness and Community Engagement
    - Role of Developer Communities: Highlight the importance of awareness and engagement of developer communities in promoting sustainable blockchains.
    - Education and Resources: Importance of education and provision of resources to support the development of eco-responsible blockchains.

7. Future Prospects
    - Upcoming Trends and Innovations: Thoughts on future trends and potential innovations in the field of eco-friendly blockchains.
    - Long-Term Impact on the Industry: Exploring the potential long-term impact of more sustainable blockchains on the blockchain industry and beyond.

Conclusion

The development of eco-friendly blockchains is essential to ensure the long-term sustainability of this revolutionary technology. By combining innovations in consensus, the use of renewable energies, technological improvements, and an adapted regulatory framework, it is possible to significantly reduce the environmental impact of blockchain. This chapter highlights the importance of a holistic and collaborative approach to developing blockchain solutions that are not only efficient and secure, but also respectful of our environment.

CHAPTER 15: CRYPTOCURRENCIES AND NATURAL RESOURCE MANAGEMENT

Introduction

The intersection between cryptocurrencies and natural resource management opens up innovative perspectives for monitoring, regulating and optimizing resource use. This chapter explores how cryptocurrency technologies, particularly blockchain, can be applied to natural resource management.

1. Blockchain and Resource Traceability
- Natural Resource Tracking: Exploring the use of blockchain for the transparent and unalterable tracking of natural resources, from their extraction to their consumption.
- Use Cases: Presentation of concrete examples where blockchain has been used to trace resources like wood, water, minerals, etc.

2. Improvement of Sustainable Management
- Certification and Sustainability Standards: Discussion on the use of blockchain to certify compliance with sustainability standards in natural resource management.
- Reducing Environmental Impact: Analysis of how blockchain can help reduce environmental impact by

optimizing the use of resources.

3. Decentralized Markets for Natural Resources
- Blockchain-Based Trading Platforms: Exploring the creation of decentralized markets for trading natural resources, increasing efficiency and transparency.
- Tokenization of Natural Resources: Discussion on the tokenization of natural resources, enabling a new form of commerce and investment.

4. Community Participation and Engagement
- Involvement of Local Communities: Analysis of the impact of blockchain on the involvement of local communities in the management of natural resources.
- Inclusive Economic Models: Exploring economic models that use blockchain to ensure more equitable distribution of benefits from natural resources.

5. Challenges and Limitations
- Technical Complexity and Accessibility: Examination of technical challenges and accessibility issues related to the use of blockchain in natural resource management.
- Governance and Regulatory Issues: Discussion on governance challenges and regulatory needs for effective blockchain integration in this area.

6. Future Perspectives and Innovations
- Emerging Technologies: Thoughts on integrating emerging technologies, such as AI and IoT, with blockchain for improved natural resource management.
- Long-Term Impact on Resource Management: Exploring the potential long-term impact of these technologies on the conservation and sustainable management of natural resources.

Conclusion

The integration of blockchain technology into natural resource management offers promising possibilities for improving traceability, sustainability and efficiency. Although facing technical and regulatory challenges, this innovative approach has the potential to transform the way natural resources are managed, traded and preserved, promoting transparency, equity and sustainability. This chapter highlights the importance of continued exploration and adoption of these technologies for a more sustainable future.

CHAPTER 16: BLOCKCHAIN IN HEALTHCARE: PRIVACY AND EFFICIENCY

Introduction

The adoption of blockchain technology in the healthcare sector promises to revolutionize medical data management in terms of privacy, security and efficiency. This chapter explores the potential applications of blockchain in healthcare and the challenges for its successful integration.

1. Challenges of Health Data Management
   - Sensitivity of Medical Data: Discussion on the sensitive nature of health data and the importance of protecting it.
   - Current Challenges: Analysis of current challenges in storing, accessing and sharing health data.

2. Blockchain for Security and Privacy
   - Encryption and Data Security: Exploring how blockchain can improve the security and privacy of medical data through its decentralized architecture and robust encryption.
   - Access Control and Patient Consent: Discussion on the use of blockchain to manage access rights to health data, giving patients increased control over their information.

3. Improved Interoperability and Access to Data
   - Data Exchange between Institutions: Analysis of the ability

of blockchain to facilitate the secure exchange of health data between different institutions and health professionals.
- Electronic Medical Records on Blockchain: Exploring the use of blockchain to create universal and easily accessible electronic medical records.

4. Applications in Drug Research and Monitoring
- Clinical Research and Trials: Discussion of using blockchain to improve data management in clinical research, including drug trials.
- Drug Traceability: Exploring the application of blockchain for tracking the drug supply chain from manufacturing to distribution.

5. Implementation Challenges
- Technical Complexity and Integration: Examination of the technical challenges and integration of blockchain into existing healthcare systems.
- Regulatory and Compliance Issues: Analysis of regulatory and compliance issues, particularly with regard to data protection legislation.

6. Future Perspectives and Innovations
- Innovation Potential in Healthcare: Thoughts on the innovation potential that blockchain could bring to the healthcare sector.
- Complementary Technologies: Discussion on integrating blockchain with other technologies, such as artificial intelligence and the Internet of Things (IoT), to improve healthcare.

Conclusion

The integration of blockchain in the healthcare sector offers promising possibilities for improving the privacy, security and efficiency of medical data management. Although facing technical and regulatory challenges, this technology has the potential to radically transform the way health data is managed, benefiting both healthcare professionals and patients. This chapter highlights the importance of continuing the development and adoption of blockchain solutions in healthcare for a safer and more efficient future in medical data management.

CHAPTER 17: USE OF CRYPTOCURRENCIES IN CONFLICT ZONES AND HUMANITARIAN CRISES

Introduction

In conflict zones and humanitarian crisis situations, traditional financial systems are often disrupted or inaccessible. Cryptocurrencies, with their decentralized nature, offer unique potential solutions. This chapter explores the use of cryptocurrencies in these difficult contexts, highlighting both opportunities and challenges.

1. Context of Conflict Zones and Humanitarian Crises
    - Financial Challenges in Conflict Zones: Examines common financial problems in conflict zones, including monetary instability and inaccessibility of banking services.
    - Urgent Humanitarian Needs: Discussion of urgent humanitarian needs and the difficulty of providing effective aid in these regions.

2. Advantages of Cryptocurrencies in These Contexts
    - Fast and Secure Fund Transfers: Exploring the ability of cryptocurrencies to facilitate fast and secure fund transfers, essential for humanitarian assistance.
    - Reducing Dependence on Local Infrastructure:

Analysis of how cryptocurrencies can reduce dependence on local financial infrastructures, which are often unstable or unreliable in conflict zones.

3. Use Cases and Real Examples
   - Humanitarian Aid Distributed via Cryptocurrencies: Presentation of real-world examples where cryptocurrencies have been used to distribute humanitarian aid.
   - Use by Affected Populations: Discussion on the use of cryptocurrencies by populations directly affected by conflicts and crises.

4. Challenges and Limitations
   - Access to Technology and the Internet: Examines the challenges related to limited access to technology and the Internet, essential for the use of cryptocurrencies.
   - Security and Volatility Issues: Analysis of concerns regarding the security of funds and the volatility of cryptocurrencies.

5. Role of NGOs and International Organizations
   - Adoption by Humanitarian Organizations: Exploring the role of NGOs and international organizations in the adoption of cryptocurrencies for humanitarian assistance.
   - Training and Awareness: Discussion on the importance of training and awareness to facilitate the use of cryptocurrencies in these contexts.

6. Future Outlook and Impact Potential
   - Future Innovations and Developments: Thoughts on future innovations in the use of cryptocurrencies for aid in conflict zones and humanitarian crises.
   - Potential Impact on Humanitarian Response: Exploring the potential long-term impact of cryptocurrencies on improving humanitarian response in crisis situations.

Conclusion

Cryptocurrencies offer unique opportunities to improve the delivery of aid in conflict zones and humanitarian crises, thanks to their speed, security and decentralized nature. However, their effective use in these contexts requires overcoming significant challenges, particularly around technological access and security. This chapter highlights the potential of cryptocurrencies to transform humanitarian response in the most difficult situations, while recognizing the need for a careful and well-informed approach.

CHAPTER 18: BLOCKCHAIN AND GOVERNANCE: ELECTRONIC VOTING AND BEYOND

Introduction

The integration of blockchain technology into governance processes promises to bring transparency, security and efficiency, particularly in the area of electronic voting. This chapter explores the potential applications of blockchain in governance, with a focus on electronic voting, while examining the challenges and implications of this technology.

1. Blockchain Principles in Governance
   - Transparency and Security with Blockchain: Introduction to the benefits of blockchain in terms of transparency and data security, essential for governance.
   - Decentralization in Decision Making: Discussion on the role of decentralization in decision making and governance.

2. Electronic Voting Based on Blockchain
   - Potential of Electronic Voting: Exploring the potential of electronic voting to improve participation and accessibility of electoral processes.
   - Security and Anonymity of Votes: Analysis of how blockchain can secure votes and preserve the anonymity of

voters.
3. Use Cases and Pilot Projects
   - Examples of Blockchain Voting Systems: Presentation of real use cases and pilot projects of blockchain-based voting systems.
   - Feedback and Lessons: Discussion on lessons learned from the first implementations of electronic voting based on blockchain.
4. Digital Identity Management
   - Digital Identities on the Blockchain: Exploring the use of blockchain for the management of digital identities, a crucial aspect for electronic voting.
   - Privacy Protection and Regulatory Compliance: Analysis of the challenges related to privacy protection and regulatory compliance in digital identity management.
5. Challenges and Limitations
   - Technical Challenges and Adoption: Examining the technical challenges and barriers to widespread adoption of blockchain-based e-voting.
   - Security and Trust Issues: Discussion of security and trust concerns in electronic voting systems.
6. Implications for Democracy and Citizen Participation
   - Impact on Citizen Participation: Reflections on the potential impact of blockchain-based electronic voting on citizen participation and democratic engagement.
   - Future of Democratic Governance: Exploring the long-term implications of blockchain adoption for democratic governance.
7. Future Perspectives and Innovations
   - Technological Developments: Reflections on future innovations in the field of electronic voting and blockchain-based governance.
   - Integration with Other Technologies: Discussion on the potential integration of blockchain with other emerging technologies to strengthen governance.

Conclusion

The use of blockchain in governance and electronic voting offers promising prospects for strengthening security, transparency and participation in democratic processes. Although facing technical and regulatory challenges, this technology has the potential to significantly transform the way decisions are made and trust is established in governance systems. This chapter highlights the importance of continuing the development and experimentation of blockchain solutions in the area of governance for a more inclusive and transparent future.

CHAPTER 19: CRYPTOCURRENCIES AND ART: BEYOND NFTS

Introduction
The intersection between cryptocurrencies and the art world extends well beyond non-fungible tokens (NFTs). This chapter explores the various ways in which cryptocurrencies influence the arts sector, in terms of financing, ownership, distribution and curation of works of art.
1. Impact of Cryptocurrencies on the Art Market
- New Forms of Funding: Exploring the ways in which cryptocurrencies offer new methods of funding for artists and artistic projects.
- Democratization of Access to Art: Analysis of the impact of cryptocurrencies on the accessibility and democratization of the purchase and collection of works of art.
2. Cryptocurrencies and Artistic Business Models
- Direct Payment to Artists: Discussion of how cryptocurrencies enable direct and transparent payment to artists for their work.
- Innovative Revenue Models: Exploring new revenue models for artists and galleries, facilitated by cryptocurrencies.
3. Beyond NFTs: Other Applications in Art
- Cryptocurrencies for Art Conservation: Examining the

use of cryptocurrencies to finance the conservation and restoration of works of art.
- Blockchain for Provenance and Authenticity: Analysis of the use of blockchain to ensure the provenance and authenticity of works of art.

4. Challenges and Limitations
- Cryptocurrency Volatility: Discussion of the challenges posed by cryptocurrency volatility in the art market.
- Legal and Copyright Issues: Exploration of legal issues, particularly copyright and intellectual property, related to the use of cryptocurrencies in art.

5. Case Studies and Successful Examples
- Artistic Projects Funded by Cryptocurrencies: Presentation of case studies where cryptocurrencies have played a key role in the financing and realization of artistic projects.
- Innovative Galleries and Exhibitions: Examples of galleries and exhibitions that integrate cryptocurrencies into their operation.

6. Future Outlook and Growth Potential
- Evolving Art and Technology Trends: Thoughts on the future evolution of trends in the intersection of art and cryptocurrencies.
- Long-Term Impact on the Art Sector: Exploring the potential long-term impact of cryptocurrencies on the arts sector, in terms of creation, distribution and conservation of art.

Conclusion

Cryptocurrencies offer exciting possibilities to transform the arts sector, providing new avenues for the financing, distribution and verification of art. Beyond NFTs, they open the way to innovative economic models and greater democratization of art. This chapter highlights the importance of carefully navigating legal and economic challenges, while embracing the opportunities that cryptocurrencies offer to enrich and diversify the art world.

CHAPTER 20: BLOCKCHAIN AND DIGITAL IDENTITY MANAGEMENT

Introduction

Digital identity management is a crucial issue in the digital age, and blockchain offers innovative solutions to meet this challenge. This chapter explores how blockchain technology can revolutionize digital identity management, ensuring security, privacy and reliability.

1. Issues of Digital Identity
   - Importance of Digital Identity: Introduction to the growing importance of digital identity in various aspects of daily and online life.
   - Current Challenges: Discussion of current challenges in security, privacy and digital identity management.

2. Blockchain for Secure Identity Management
   - Blockchain Principles in Identity Management: Exploring how blockchain can provide a secure, decentralized platform for digital identity management.
   - Benefits in terms of Security and Privacy: Analysis of the benefits of blockchain in terms of protecting personal data and preventing identity fraud.

3. Practical Applications
   - Authentication and Identity Verification: Introducing practical applications of blockchain for authentication and

identity verification in various industries, such as finance, healthcare, and e-commerce.
- Access and Authorization Management: Discussion of using blockchain to manage access and authorization in a secure and transparent manner.

4. Data Sovereignty and User Control
- User Empowerment: Exploring how blockchain allows users to control their own identity data.
- Data Portability: Analysis of the portability of digital identity data thanks to blockchain, facilitating their use across different services and platforms.

5. Challenges and Limitations
- Technical Complexity and Adoption: Examining the technical challenges and barriers to widespread adoption of blockchain-based identity management.
- Regulatory and Compliance Issues: Discussion of regulatory and compliance issues related to the use of blockchain for digital identity management.

6. Future Perspectives and Innovations
- Technological Developments and Trends: Thoughts on future developments in blockchain in digital identity management and emerging trends in this area.
- Integration with Other Technologies: Exploring the potential integration of blockchain with other technologies, such as artificial intelligence and the Internet of Things (IoT), to improve identity management.

Conclusion

Blockchain has significant potential to transform digital identity management, providing a more secure, private and user-controlled solution. Although facing technical and regulatory challenges, this technology promises to bring significant changes to the way digital identities are managed and used across various industries. This chapter highlights the importance of continued development and innovation in this area to fully realize the potential of blockchain in digital identity management.

CHAPTER 21: AI FOR CRYPTOCURRENCY MARKET PREDICTION

Introduction

Artificial intelligence (AI) is playing an increasingly crucial role in analyzing and predicting cryptocurrency markets. This chapter explores how AI is used to understand and anticipate cryptocurrency market movements, highlighting the opportunities and challenges associated with this technology.

1. Foundations of AI in Finance
   - Principles of AI in Finance: Introduction to the basic concepts of AI and its application in the financial field.
   - History of AI in Market Prediction: Brief history of the use of AI for financial market prediction and its evolution towards cryptocurrencies.

2. AI in Cryptocurrency Analysis
   - Predictive Models and Algorithms: Exploring the different AI models and algorithms used to analyze and predict cryptocurrency markets.
   - Technical and Fundamental Analysis: Discussion on the application of AI to the technical and fundamental analysis of cryptocurrencies.

3. Data Processing and Machine Learning
   - Big Data Management: Analysis of how AI manages and processes the vast amounts of data generated by cryptocurrency markets.

- Machine Learning and Modeling: Exploring the use of machine learning to develop predictive models in cryptocurrency trading.

4. Practical Applications of AI
   - Algorithmic Trading: Overview of AI-based algorithmic trading systems for cryptocurrencies.
   - Risk Management and Portfolio Optimization: Discussion on the use of AI for risk management and optimization of cryptocurrency portfolios.

5. Challenges and Limitations
   - Volatility and Predictability: Examines the challenges posed by the volatility inherent in cryptocurrency markets and the impact on the accuracy of AI predictions.
   - Ethical and Regulatory Issues: Analysis of ethical and regulatory issues related to the use of AI in cryptocurrency trading.

6. Future Perspectives and Innovations
   - Technological Developments in AI: Thoughts on future innovations and emerging trends in the application of AI to cryptocurrency markets.
   - Potential Impact on Cryptocurrency Trading: Exploring the potential long-term impact of AI on trading strategies and cryptocurrency market dynamics.

Conclusion

The use of AI for cryptocurrency market prediction offers exciting possibilities for traders and investors, enabling deeper analysis and more informed trading decisions. Although facing challenges in terms of volatility and regulation, AI continues to evolve and promises to play an increasingly important role in cryptocurrency trading strategy. This chapter highlights the importance of continued innovation and caution in using AI to navigate the ever-changing cryptocurrency markets.

CHAPTER 22: SELF-SCALING SMART CONTRACTS USING AI

Introduction

The integration of artificial intelligence (AI) into smart contracts paves the way for self-evolving smart contracts, capable of dynamically adapting and responding to changing conditions and environments. This chapter explores the potential and implications of this fusion between AI and blockchain in the development of advanced smart contracts.

1. Foundations of Smart Contracts and AI
- Principles of Smart Contracts: Introduction to smart contracts, their operation and their current applications.
- Role of AI in Smart Contracts: Exploring how AI can be integrated into smart contracts to improve their functionality and effectiveness.

2. Development of Self-Evolving Smart Contracts
- Characteristics of Self-Evolving Smart Contracts: Description of the unique characteristics of self-evolving smart contracts, including adaptability and autonomous decision-making.
- AI Technologies Involved: Analysis of specific AI technologies used to develop self-evolving smart contracts, such as machine learning and natural language processing.

3. Applications and Use Cases
- Dynamic Contract Management: Presentation of the practical applications of self-evolving smart contracts,

particularly in the dynamic management of contracts according to market or regulatory changes.
- Automation in Various Sectors: Exploring the use of these smart contracts in various sectors, such as finance, supply chain and public administration.

4. Benefits and Improvements
- Efficiency and Error Reduction: Discussion of how self-evolving smart contracts can increase efficiency and reduce human errors.
- Responsiveness and Flexibility: Analysis of the ability of these contracts to respond quickly and flexibly to changing conditions.

5. Challenges and Ethical Considerations
- Complexity and Reliability: Examining the challenges related to the increased complexity of self-evolving smart contracts and their reliability.
- Ethical and Security Issues: Exploring ethical implications and security concerns, particularly as they relate to autonomous decision-making by AI.

6. Future Outlook and Potential Impact
- Future Innovations in AI and Smart Contracts: Thoughts on future innovations and the evolution of self-evolving smart contracts using AI.
- Impact on Law and Regulation: Discussion on the potential impact of these technologies on legal and regulatory frameworks.

Conclusion

Self-evolving smart contracts represent a significant advancement in blockchain and AI, offering unprecedented possibilities for automation and adaptability. Although promising, they raise technical, ethical and regulatory challenges that must be carefully addressed. This chapter highlights the importance of continuous innovation and interdisciplinary collaboration to fully exploit the potential of self-evolving smart contracts, while navigating their complexities and implications.

CHAPTER 23: AI AND FRAUD RISK ANALYSIS IN CRYPTOCURRENCIES

Introduction

With the rise of cryptocurrencies, the risks of fraud and financial embezzlement have increased, requiring sophisticated solutions for their detection and prevention. Artificial intelligence (AI) offers powerful tools to analyze and mitigate these risks. This chapter explores the application of AI in fraud detection in the cryptocurrency ecosystem.

1. Context of Cryptocurrency Fraud
   - Nature of Cryptocurrency Fraud: Introduction to the types of fraud commonly encountered in the cryptocurrency space, including phishing, wallet hacks and trading scams.
   - Fraud Detection Challenges: Discussion of the unique challenges posed by the cryptocurrency ecosystem for fraud detection.
2. Role of AI in Fraud Detection
   - AI Technologies for Financial Security: Exploring different AI technologies used to detect fraudulent activity, such as machine learning and data analytics.
   - Predictive Models and Pattern Recognition: Analysis of how AI can identify suspicious transaction patterns and predict potential fraud risks.
3. Monitoring and Alert Systems

- Real-Time Monitoring: Introducing AI-based real-time monitoring systems to monitor transactions and activities on cryptocurrency exchanges.
- Alert and Response Mechanisms: Discussion of automatic alert mechanisms and response protocols in the event of suspicious activity detection.

4. Behavioral Analysis and Profiling
- User and Transaction Profiling: Exploring the use of AI to profile user behaviors and identify deviations from normal patterns.
- Behavior-Based Fraud Prevention: Analysis of how behavioral analysis can help prevent fraud by identifying suspicious behavior.

5. Challenges and Limitations of AI
- False Positives and Model Accuracy: Examining the challenges of false positives and the need to balance the sensitivity and specificity of AI models.
- Ethical and Privacy Issues: Discussion of the ethical implications and privacy issues related to the use of AI for transaction monitoring and analysis.

6. Future Perspectives and Developments
- Technological Improvements and Innovations: Thoughts on future improvements and innovations in the application of AI to cryptocurrency fraud detection.
- Regulatory and Industry Collaboration: Exploring the importance of collaboration between regulators, cryptocurrency businesses and AI developers for an effective approach to fraud prevention.

Conclusion

The use of AI to analyze and mitigate fraud risks in cryptocurrencies is a growing field, offering promising solutions for securing digital assets. Although facing technical and ethical challenges, AI represents an indispensable tool for navigating the complex and rapidly evolving landscape of cryptocurrency fraud. This chapter highlights the importance of continuous innovation and strategic collaboration to strengthen security in the cryptocurrency ecosystem.

CHAPTER 24: DEVELOPMENT OF AI-MANAGED CRYPTOCURRENCIES

Introduction

The integration of artificial intelligence (AI) into the management and operation of cryptocurrencies represents a significant advance in the field of digital finance. This chapter explores the possibilities and challenges associated with the development of AI-driven cryptocurrencies, focusing on their potential to revolutionize the cryptocurrency market.

1. Foundations of AI in Cryptocurrency Management
   - Role of AI in Digital Finance: Introduction to the growing importance of AI in the financial sector, particularly in digital asset management.
   - Potential Applications of AI in Cryptocurrencies: Exploring the different ways in which AI can be integrated into cryptocurrency management.

2. Cryptocurrencies Managed by AI
   - Automation of Trading Decisions: Analysis of AI's ability to automate trading decisions, optimizing buy and sell strategies.
   - Dynamic Portfolio Management: Discussion of the use of AI for dynamic portfolio management, adjusting investments based on changing market conditions.

3. AI Algorithms and Market Analysis

- Predictive Models: Introducing AI-based predictive models to anticipate cryptocurrency market trends.
- Market Data Analysis: Exploring the use of AI to analyze large amounts of market data, including social and economic signals.

4. Security and Regulation
- Fraud and Anomaly Detection: Examining the ability of AI to detect fraudulent activity and anomalies in cryptocurrency transactions.
- Regulatory Compliance: Discussion on the use of AI to ensure compliance with financial regulations and cryptocurrency laws.

5. Challenges and Limitations
- Technical Complexity and Reliability: Analysis of the technical challenges associated with the development of AI-driven cryptocurrencies, including issues of reliability and prediction accuracy.
- Ethical and Transparency Issues: Exploring ethical and transparency concerns related to the use of AI in cryptocurrency management.

6. Future Perspectives and Innovations
- Technological Developments in AI and Cryptocurrencies: Thoughts on future innovations and emerging trends in the intersection of AI and cryptocurrencies.
- Potential Impact on the Cryptocurrency Market: Exploring the potential long-term impact of AI-managed cryptocurrencies on the overall cryptocurrency market.

Conclusion

The development of AI-managed cryptocurrencies represents an exciting frontier in digital finance, offering opportunities for increased automation, efficiency and security. Although facing technical and ethical challenges, these innovations promise to transform the way cryptocurrency markets operate and are managed. This chapter highlights the importance of continuous innovation and interdisciplinary collaboration to fully exploit the potential of AI-managed cryptocurrencies.

CHAPTER 25: AI AND BLOCKCHAIN NETWORK OPTIMIZATION

Introduction

The integration of artificial intelligence (AI) into blockchain networks offers opportunities to improve their efficiency, security and scalability. This chapter explores how AI can be used to optimize blockchain networks, focusing on the innovations and challenges associated with this integration.

1. Synergy between AI and Blockchain
   - Complementarity of AI and Blockchain: Introduction to the benefits of combining AI with blockchain technology, emphasizing their complementary strengths.
   - Potential Applications of AI in Blockchain: Exploring the different ways AI can be integrated into blockchain networks to improve their performance.

2. Optimization of Network Performance
   - Improving Transaction Efficiency: Analysis of how AI can optimize the processing and validation of transactions on the blockchain.
   - Resource Management and Allocation: Discussion of the use of AI for more efficient management of resources within blockchain networks, including the allocation of computing power.

3. AI-Enhanced Security
- Threat and Anomaly Detection: Overview of AI-based systems for early detection of threats and abnormal behavior in blockchain networks.
- Automated Responses to Security Incidents: Exploring the use of AI to automate responses to security incidents, thereby improving network resilience.

4. Scalability and Data Management
- Scalability Optimization: Analysis of AI strategies to improve the scalability of blockchain networks, addressing bottlenecks and optimizing consensus protocols.
- Intelligent Data Management: Discussion on the use of AI for more efficient management of data stored on the blockchain, including data compression and archiving.

5. Challenges and Limitations
- Complexity and Implementation Costs: Examines the challenges of integrating AI into blockchain networks, including technical complexity and associated costs.
- Ethical and Privacy Issues: Exploring ethical concerns and privacy issues related to the use of AI in blockchain network management.

6. Future Perspectives and Innovations
- Technological Developments and Trends: Thoughts on future innovations and emerging trends in the integration of AI into blockchain networks.
- Potential Impact on the Blockchain Ecosystem: Exploring the potential long-term impact of AI optimization of blockchain networks on the entire blockchain ecosystem.

Conclusion

The integration of AI into blockchain networks represents a promising step forward to improve their efficiency, security and scalability. Although facing technical and ethical challenges, this combination offers significant opportunities for innovation and improvement for the future of blockchain technologies. This chapter highlights the importance of continued exploration and careful adoption of AI in blockchain networks to fully realize its potential.

CHAPTER 26: CRYPTOCURRENCIES IN SPACE: FINANCING AND LOGISTICS OF SPACE MISSIONS

Introduction
Space exploration is entering a new era with the integration of cryptocurrencies, offering innovative solutions for the financing and logistics of space missions. This chapter examines how cryptocurrencies and blockchain technology can transform the space sector, focusing on the associated opportunities and challenges.

1. Context of Space Exploration and Cryptocurrencies
- Evolution of Space Exploration: Brief history of space exploration and its financing.
- Introduction of Cryptocurrencies into Space: Exploration of the entry of cryptocurrencies into the space domain and their disruptive potential.

2. Financing Space Missions with Cryptocurrencies
- Crowdfunding and Investments: Analysis of the use of cryptocurrencies for crowdfunding and investments in space projects.
- Tokenization of Space Projects: Discussion on the tokenization of space assets and missions to facilitate

financing.

3. Blockchain for Space Logistics
- Supply Chain Management: Exploring the use of blockchain for supply chain management in space missions, from manufacturing to orbit.
- Asset Tracking and Security: Analysis of the application of blockchain for the secure tracking of space equipment and technologies.

4. Cryptocurrencies and Space Economy
- Transactions and Exchanges in Space: Discussion of the potential role of cryptocurrencies in economic transactions and exchanges in space.
- Development of a Sustainable Space Economy: Exploring the implications of cryptocurrencies for the development of a sustainable and autonomous space economy.

5. Challenges and Limitations
- Technical and Regulatory Challenges: Examination of the technical and regulatory challenges related to the use of cryptocurrencies and blockchain in space.
- Security and Volatility Issues: Analysis of transaction security concerns and volatility of cryptocurrencies in the spatial context.

6. Future Perspectives and Innovations
- Technological Innovations and Collaboration: Reflections on future innovations in the use of cryptocurrencies and blockchain for space exploration.
- Public-Private Partnerships and International Cooperation: Discussion on the importance of public-private partnerships and international cooperation to integrate cryptocurrencies into the space economy.

Conclusion

The integration of cryptocurrencies in space exploration opens new horizons for the financing and management of space missions. By offering innovative solutions for economic and logistical challenges, cryptocurrencies have the potential to play a key role in the future space economy. This chapter highlights the importance of continued innovation and cross-sector collaboration to fully harness the potential of cryptocurrencies in advancing space exploration.

CHAPTER 27: BLOCKCHAIN AND INTERNET OF THINGS (IOT): CREATING AUTONOMOUS ECONOMIES

Introduction

The intersection of blockchain and the Internet of Things (IoT) represents a major step forward toward creating self-sustaining economies. This chapter explores how the combination of these two technologies can transform interactions between connected devices and automate business processes.

1. Fundamentals of IoT and Blockchain
- IoT Principles: Introduction to the basic concepts of the Internet of Things and its role in modern connectivity.
- Blockchain in IoT: Exploring the application of blockchain in IoT to secure data and transactions between devices.

2. Creation of Autonomous Economies
- Transaction Automation: Analysis of how blockchain can automate transactions and interactions between IoT devices.
- IoT-Based Autonomous Economies: Discussion of creating autonomous economies where IoT devices interact and

transact independently.
3. Security and Data Management
- Blockchain-Enhanced Security: Exploring the use of blockchain to strengthen the security of IoT networks and protect against cyberattacks.
- Transparent Data Management: Analysis of the blockchain's ability to offer transparent and decentralized management of data generated by IoT devices.
4. Use Cases and Practical Applications
- Smart Cities and Energy Management: Presentation of applications of the blockchain-IoT combination in smart cities, particularly for intelligent energy management.
- Supply Chain and Logistics: Discussion on the application of this technology in the supply chain to improve traceability and efficiency.
5. Challenges and Limitations
- Technical Complexity and Integration: Examination of the technical challenges related to integrating blockchain with IoT.
- Scalability and Resource Management: Analysis of scalability and resource management issues in wide-area IoT networks.
6. Future Perspectives and Innovations
- Technological Developments: Thoughts on future innovations in the integration of blockchain and IoT.
- Potential Impact on Industries and Society: Exploring the potential impact of these technologies on various industries and society as a whole.

Conclusion

The merger of blockchain and IoT paves the way for autonomous and intelligent economies, where connected devices can interact and transact securely and efficiently. Although facing technical and scalability challenges, this combination promises to transform many industries by automating processes and improving data security and transparency. This chapter highlights the importance of continuous innovation and cross-sector collaboration to fully harness the potential of blockchain and IoT in creating self-sustaining economies.

CHAPTER 28: CRYPTOCURRENCIES AND THE QUANTUM ECONOMY: PREPARING FOR THE FUTURE

Introduction

The advent of quantum technology presents both opportunities and challenges for the world of cryptocurrencies. This chapter explores the potential impact of quantum computing on cryptocurrencies and how the industry is preparing for this new technological era.

1. Foundations of Quantum Computing
   - Principles of Quantum Computing: Introduction to the basic concepts of quantum computing, including superposition and quantum entanglement.
   - Evolution and Current Status of Quantum Technology: Overview of the evolution of quantum computing and its current status.

2. Impact of Quantum Computing on Cryptocurrencies
   - Threats to Cryptographic Security: Analysis of the threats that quantum computing poses to current cryptographic security, particularly to the cryptographic algorithms upon

which many cryptocurrencies are based.
- Challenges for Blockchain and Cryptocurrencies: Discussion of the specific challenges that quantum computing presents for blockchain and cryptocurrencies.

3. Preparation and Adaptation to Quantum
- Post-Quantum Cryptography: Exploring developments in post-quantum cryptography designed to resist quantum computing attacks.
- Updating Blockchain Protocols: Analysis of strategies for updating blockchain protocols to make them resistant to quantum threats.

4. Opportunities Offered by Quantum Computing
- Improving Computational Capabilities: Discussion of how quantum computing could improve computational capabilities for transactions and smart contracts.
- Innovations in Finance and Beyond: Exploring the potential innovations that quantum computing could bring to finance and technology.

5. Challenges and Limitations
- Complexity and Costs of Quantum Computing: Examines the challenges associated with the complexity and high costs of quantum computing.
- Ethical and Security Issues: Analysis of ethical issues and security concerns related to the adoption of quantum computing.

6. Future Outlook and Preparation
- Evolution of Quantum Computing: Reflections on the future evolution of quantum computing and its gradual integration into the cryptocurrency sector.
- Preparing Strategies for the Quantum Era: Discussion of strategies that cryptocurrency industry players can adopt to prepare for the era of quantum computing.

Conclusion

Quantum computing represents a turning point for the cryptocurrency industry, providing both security challenges and opportunities for innovation. Preparing for this new technological era is essential to ensure the security, viability and effectiveness of cryptocurrencies in the future. This chapter highlights the importance of proactive adaptation and continuous innovation to navigate the changing landscape of digital finance in the quantum era.

CHAPTER 29: EXPLORING CRYPTOCURRENCIES IN VIRTUAL WORLDS AND METAVERSES

Introduction

The emergence of virtual worlds and the metaverse is creating new frontiers for the use of cryptocurrencies. This chapter examines how cryptocurrencies are integrated into these digital spaces, focusing on their role in transactions, digital ownership, and the virtual economy.

1. Virtual Worlds and the Metaverse
   - Definition and Evolution of the Metaverse: Introduction to the concepts of virtual worlds and the metaverse, and their rapid evolution.
   - Economic Importance of Virtual Worlds: Discussion of the growing importance of virtual worlds and the metaverse in the digital economy.

2. Cryptocurrencies in the Metaverse
   - Role of Cryptocurrencies: Analysis of the role of cryptocurrencies in transactions within virtual worlds, including the purchase of virtual goods and services.
   - Cryptocurrency Integration: Exploring how cryptocurrencies are integrated into metaverse platforms to

facilitate economic exchange.
3. Digital Property and NFTs
- NFTs in the Metaverse: Discussion of the use of non-fungible tokens (NFTs) to represent ownership of unique digital assets in virtual worlds.
- NFT Markets and the Virtual Economy: Analysis of NFT markets in the metaverse and their impact on the virtual economy.

4. Development of Virtual Economies
- Creating Autonomous Economies: Exploring the creation of autonomous economies within virtual worlds, supported by cryptocurrencies.
- Economic Challenges and Opportunities: Discussion of the challenges and opportunities associated with the development of virtual economies based on cryptocurrencies.

5. Security and Regulatory Challenges
- Transaction Security: Examination of the security challenges associated with the use of cryptocurrencies in virtual worlds.
- Regulatory Issues: Analysis of emerging regulatory and legal issues regarding cryptocurrency transactions in the metaverse.

6. Future Perspectives and Innovations
- Technological Developments and Trends: Reflections on future developments in virtual worlds and the metaverse, and the continued integration of cryptocurrencies.
- Impact on Industries and Society: Exploring the potential impact of virtual worlds and cryptocurrencies on various industries and society as a whole.

Conclusion

The integration of cryptocurrencies into virtual worlds and the metaverse represents an exciting development in the digital economy. It offers unique possibilities for digital ownership, commerce and the creation of self-sustaining virtual economies.

This chapter highlights the importance of carefully navigating security and regulatory challenges, while embracing the opportunities that cryptocurrencies offer to enrich and diversify experiences in virtual worlds.

CHAPTER 30: PROSPECTIVE: CRYPTOCURRENCIES IN 50 YEARS

Introduction
Considering the future of cryptocurrencies over a 50-year horizon involves exploring futuristic scenarios, marked by technological advances, economic changes and societal developments. This chapter looks at possible projections for cryptocurrencies, taking into account current trends and potential innovations.

1. Technological Evolution and Adoption
- Future Innovations: Exploring possible technological advancements in cryptocurrencies, including quantum computing and AI.
- Widespread Adoption: Discussion of the scenario of widespread adoption of cryptocurrencies, influencing global financial systems and daily transactions.

2. Integration into the Global Economy
- Cryptocurrencies and Financial Systems: Analysis of the potential integration of cryptocurrencies into traditional financial systems and their impact on overall monetary policy.
- Role in International Trade: Exploring the role of cryptocurrencies in international trade, trade facilitation and the impact on emerging economies.

3. Innovations in Governance Models
- Decentralized Governance: Discussion on the evolution towards more decentralized governance models, facilitated by blockchain and cryptocurrencies.
- Cryptocurrencies and Public Policies: Analysis of the impact of cryptocurrencies on public policies, including taxation and regulation.

4. Societal and Cultural Impact
- Changing Social Norms: Exploring the impact of cryptocurrencies on social and cultural norms, including perceptions of value and ownership.
- Financial Inclusion and Social Change: Discussion on the potential of cryptocurrencies to promote financial inclusion and drive social change.

5. Future Challenges and Risks
- Security and Stability: Examination of future challenges related to the security and stability of cryptocurrencies, taking into account technological advances.
- Ethical and Environmental Issues: Analysis of persistent ethical and environmental concerns related to the use of cryptocurrencies.

6. Futuristic Scenarios
- Cryptocurrencies and Emerging Technologies: Thoughts on the interaction of cryptocurrencies with other emerging technologies, such as IoT and the metaverse.
- Long-Term Vision: Exploring futuristic scenarios where cryptocurrencies could radically transform aspects of daily life, economics and governance.

Conclusion

Looking at the future of cryptocurrencies over half a century opens up a field of fascinating possibilities, marked by technological advances, profound economic changes and significant societal impacts. While the exact future remains uncertain, it is clear that cryptocurrencies have the potential to play a major role in shaping our future world. This chapter invites reflection on the opportunities, challenges and responsibilities that accompany this continued evolution.

Exploration of avenues of reflection

CHAPTER 31: LEGAL AND REGULATORY ASPECTS OF CRYPTOCURRENCIES

Introduction
The rise of cryptocurrencies has attracted increased attention from regulators and lawmakers around the world. This chapter explores the legal and regulatory aspects of cryptocurrencies, focusing on the challenges and developments in this area.

1. Global Regulatory Overview
- Diversity of Regulatory Frameworks: Introduction to the diversity of regulatory approaches adopted by different countries towards cryptocurrencies.
- International Regulatory Trends: Analysis of international regulatory trends, including coordinated regulatory initiatives.

2. Regulation of Cryptocurrency Exchanges
- Licensing and Compliance: Discussion of licensing and compliance requirements for cryptocurrency exchanges.
- Anti-Money Laundering (AML) and KYC Measures: Exploration of AML (Anti-Money Laundering) and KYC (Know Your Customer) regulations applied to cryptocurrency exchanges.

3. Taxation of Cryptocurrencies
- Taxation of Cryptocurrencies: Analysis of tax policies

regarding cryptocurrencies in different countries.
- Tax Reporting and Compliance: Discussion of the challenges and obligations related to reporting cryptocurrency transactions to tax authorities.

4. Regulation of ICOs and Tokens
- Legal Framework for ICOs: Exploring the legal aspects of Initial Coin Offerings (ICOs) and their regulation.
- Classification of Tokens: Analysis of the different classifications of tokens (utility, security, etc.) and their regulatory implications.

5. Cryptocurrencies and Financial Institutions
- Integration into the Traditional Financial System: Discussion on the integration of cryptocurrencies into the traditional financial system and the associated regulatory challenges.
- Financial Regulatory Standards: Analysis of the application of existing financial regulatory standards to cryptocurrencies.

6. Legal and Regulatory Challenges
- Balancing Innovation and Regulation: Examining the challenges in balancing the promotion of innovation and the protection of investors.
- Cross-Border Jurisdiction and Legislation Issues: Exploring the jurisdictional complexities and cross-border law issues related to cryptocurrencies.

7. Future Perspectives and Regulatory Developments
- Future Regulatory Developments: Thoughts on future regulatory developments and their potential impact on the cryptocurrency ecosystem.
- Stakeholder Dialogue: Discussion on the importance of dialogue between regulators, cryptocurrency businesses and users to shape an effective regulatory framework.

Conclusion

The legal and regulatory aspects of cryptocurrencies represent a complex and constantly evolving area, requiring continued attention from market participants, regulators and legislators. As the cryptocurrency landscape continues to mature, a balanced and informed approach is essential to ensuring the security, transparency and stability of this growing ecosystem. This chapter highlights the importance of thoughtful regulation that supports innovation while protecting the interests of users and the overall financial system.

CHAPTER 32: IMPACT OF CRYPTOCURRENCIES ON TRADITIONAL BANKS AND THE FINANCIAL SYSTEM

Introduction
The emergence of cryptocurrencies represents a challenge and an opportunity for traditional banks and the global financial system. This chapter explores the impact of cryptocurrencies on these institutions, analyzing the changes they bring and possible responses from the banking sector.

1. Disruption of the Traditional Banking Model
   - Decentralization of Finance: Discussion of how the decentralized nature of cryptocurrencies challenges the centralized model of traditional banks.
   - Reduction of Transaction Fees: Analysis of the impact of cryptocurrencies on the reduction of transaction fees, a traditionally lucrative area for banks.

2. Cryptocurrencies and Banking Services
   - New Services and Products: Exploring new services and products that banks could offer to integrate cryptocurrencies, such as cryptocurrency accounts and

advisory services.
- Adoption of Blockchain Technology: Analysis of the adoption of blockchain technology by banks to improve the efficiency and security of transactions.

3. Impact on International Payments and Transfers
- Simplifying International Payments: Discussion of how cryptocurrencies can simplify and speed up international payments.
- Competition with Established Payment Systems: Analysis of the impact of cryptocurrencies on established payment systems and their potential to replace or complement them.

4. Regulatory Responses and Adaptation
- Central Bank Regulatory Responses: Exploring central bank regulatory responses to cryptocurrencies, including the development of central bank digital currencies (CBDCs).
- Adaptation of Traditional Banks: Discussion on the adaptation strategies of traditional banks in the face of the rise of cryptocurrencies.

5. Security and Compliance Challenges
- Security Risk Management: Examination of the security challenges associated with the integration of cryptocurrencies into banking services.
- Compliance and Anti-Money Laundering: Analysis of compliance issues, particularly in the fight against money laundering and terrorist financing.

6. Future Outlook and Developments in the Sector
- Evolution of the Banking Landscape: Reflections on the future evolution of the banking landscape in the era of cryptocurrencies.
- Innovations and Collaborations: Exploring potential innovations and collaboration opportunities between traditional banks and cryptocurrency businesses.

Conclusion

Cryptocurrencies represent both a challenge and an opportunity for the traditional financial system. As these digital currencies gain popularity and acceptance, banks and financial institutions are called upon to adapt, innovate and rethink their business models. This chapter highlights the importance for the banking sector to remain agile and receptive to technological developments to remain relevant in a financial future increasingly dominated by cryptocurrencies.

CHAPTER 33: CRYPTOCURRENCY EDUCATION AND AWARENESS

Introduction

As cryptocurrencies grow in popularity, education and awareness become crucial to ensure proper understanding and use of this technology. This chapter discusses the importance of education and awareness in the field of cryptocurrencies, with an emphasis on strategies to improve knowledge among the general public and investors.

1. Importance of Cryptocurrency Education
   - Basic Understanding of Cryptocurrencies: Discussion on the importance of a basic understanding of cryptocurrencies for the general public.
   - Demystifying Blockchain Technology: Analysis of the need to demystify blockchain technology and how it works.
2. Education Programs and Initiatives
   - Educational Initiatives: Presentation of existing educational initiatives, including online courses, workshops and seminars.
   - Role of Educational Institutions: Exploring the role of schools, universities and other educational institutions in providing formal education about cryptocurrencies.
3. Risk and Safety Awareness

- Investment Risks: Discussion on raising awareness of the risks associated with investing in cryptocurrencies.
- Cryptocurrency Security: Analysis of security best practices for cryptocurrency portfolio management and fraud protection.

4. Education for Regulation and Compliance
- Knowledge of Regulatory Frameworks: Exploring the importance of understanding the regulatory frameworks and tax obligations related to cryptocurrencies.
- Training for Professionals: Discussion of specific training for professionals, including financial advisors, accountants and lawyers.

5. Challenges in Cryptocurrency Education
- Technical Complexity: Examining the challenges posed by the technical complexity of cryptocurrencies and how to simplify them for better understanding.
- Rapid Evolution of the Field: Analysis of the difficulty of keeping educational programs up to date with the rapid evolution of the cryptocurrency field.

6. Future Prospects and Resource Development
- Innovative Educational Resources: Reflections on the development of innovative educational resources, including the use of augmented and virtual reality.
- Importance of Continuing Education: Discussion on the importance of continuing education to stay informed of the latest developments and innovations in the field of cryptocurrencies.

Conclusion

Education and awareness play a crucial role in the adoption and secure use of cryptocurrencies. By providing accessible educational resources and raising public awareness of the risks, benefits and best practices, it is possible to create a solid foundation for the future of cryptocurrencies. This chapter highlights the importance of a proactive and inclusive approach to education to enable a wider audience to safely participate in the

NICOLASMAJEUR

cryptocurrency economy.

CHAPTER 34: CRYPTOCURRENCIES AND FINANCIAL INCLUSION

Introduction

Financial inclusion, which aims to make financial services accessible to all segments of society, is a key objective in global economic development. Cryptocurrencies, with their decentralized and accessible nature, offer unique opportunities to promote financial inclusion. This chapter explores the role of cryptocurrencies in improving access to financial services, particularly for unbanked and underbanked populations.

1. Challenges of Financial Inclusion
   - Barriers to Financial Access: Discussion of traditional barriers to accessing financial services, such as high costs, limited infrastructure and regulatory requirements.
   - Impact on Underbanked Populations: Analysis of the impact of financial exclusion on underbanked populations, particularly in developing regions.
2. Potential of Cryptocurrencies for Financial Inclusion
   - Easy Access to Financial Services: Exploring how cryptocurrencies can provide easy and inexpensive access to financial services.
   - Simplified Cross-Border Transactions: Analysis of the impact of cryptocurrencies on the simplification of cross-

border transactions, reducing costs and delays.

3. Use Cases and Real Examples
- Examples of Financial Inclusion Projects: Presentation of real use cases where cryptocurrencies have been used to promote financial inclusion.
- Pilot Programs and Initiatives: Discussion on various pilot programs and initiatives aimed at using cryptocurrencies for financial inclusion in different regions.

4. Complementary Technologies
- Mobile Banking and Cryptocurrencies: Exploring the interaction between mobile banking and cryptocurrencies, and their role in improving access to financial services.
- Blockchain for Transparency and Security: Analysis of the use of blockchain technology to ensure transparency and security in financial services.

5. Challenges and Limitations
- Cryptocurrency Volatility: Examining the challenges posed by cryptocurrency volatility and their impact on financial inclusion.
- Education and Awareness: Discussion on the importance of education and awareness to facilitate the adoption of cryptocurrencies in underbanked populations.

6. Future Perspectives and Policies
- Regulatory and Policy Developments: Reflections on the regulatory and policy developments necessary to support the use of cryptocurrencies in financial inclusion.
- Cross-Sector Collaboration: Exploring the need for collaboration between the public and private sectors to promote financial inclusion through cryptocurrencies.

Conclusion

Cryptocurrencies have the potential to play a significant role in promoting financial inclusion, by providing simplified and cheaper access to financial services. To fully realize this potential, it is essential to overcome challenges related to volatility, education and regulation. This chapter highlights the importance of a holistic and collaborative approach to integrating cryptocurrencies into financial inclusion strategies, with a view to creating a financial system that is more inclusive and accessible to all.

CHAPTER 35: SUSTAINABLE DEVELOPMENT AND CRYPTOCURRENCIES

Introduction

Sustainable development, focused on meeting the needs of the present without compromising the ability of future generations to meet their own needs, is a crucial global issue. Cryptocurrencies, as an emerging technology, present both challenges and opportunities for sustainable development. This chapter explores the intersection between cryptocurrencies and sustainable development, focusing on their environmental, economic and social impact.

1. Environmental Impact of Cryptocurrencies
   - Energy Consumption of Mining: Analysis of the environmental impact of energy consumption linked to the mining of cryptocurrencies, in particular for currencies based on the Proof of Work system.
   - Initiatives to Reduce the Carbon Footprint: Exploring initiatives to reduce the carbon footprint of cryptocurrencies, including the use of renewable energy and the development of more energy efficient protocols.

2. Cryptocurrencies and the Circular Economy
   - Tokenization of Resources and Environmental Rights: Discussion of the use of cryptocurrencies and tokens to

represent and exchange resources and environmental rights.
- Promoting Transparency and Traceability: Analysis of how blockchain can promote transparency and traceability in supply chains, thereby contributing to a more circular economy.

3. Financial Inclusion and Economic Development
- Access to Financial Services in Underdeveloped Regions: Exploring the role of cryptocurrencies in improving access to financial services in underdeveloped regions, thereby promoting economic development.
- Support for Small Businesses and Entrepreneurs: Discussion on how cryptocurrencies can support small businesses and entrepreneurs, particularly in emerging economies.

4. Cryptocurrencies and Social Responsibility
- Cryptocurrencies for Social and Humanitarian Initiatives: Analysis of the use of cryptocurrencies to finance social and humanitarian initiatives, including charitable donations and crowdfunding campaigns.
- Ethics and Governance in the Cryptocurrency Ecosystem: Discussion on the importance of ethics and good governance in the cryptocurrency ecosystem to ensure sustainable development.

5. Challenges and Limitations
- Regulatory and Compliance Challenges: Examination of the regulatory and compliance challenges related to the use of cryptocurrencies in the context of sustainable development.
- Awareness and Education: Analysis of the need for increased awareness and education on the impact of cryptocurrencies on sustainable development.

6. Future Perspectives and Innovations
- Technological Innovations for Sustainability: Reflections on future technological innovations in the field of cryptocurrencies that could promote sustainable development.
- Cross-Sector Collaborations: Exploring the importance of

collaborations between the public and private sectors, as well as non-governmental organizations, to promote sustainable development through cryptocurrencies.

Conclusion

Cryptocurrencies, as a disruptive technology, have the potential to play a significant role in promoting sustainable development. However, to realize this potential, it is crucial to address the environmental, economic and social challenges they present. This chapter highlights the need for a balanced and innovative approach to integrating cryptocurrencies into sustainable development strategies, with a view to creating a greener, more inclusive and more equitable future.

CHAPTER 36: CRYPTOCURRENCIES AND MONETARY POLICY

Introduction

The emergence of cryptocurrencies raises important questions about their interaction with traditional monetary policy. This chapter explores the impact of cryptocurrencies on the monetary policy of nations, examining how they can influence established financial systems and central bank decisions.

1. Foundations of Monetary Policy
   - Principles of Monetary Policy: Introduction to the basic concepts of monetary policy, including the regulation of money supply and the control of interest rates.
   - Role of Central Banks: Discussion on the traditional role of central banks in the management of monetary policy.

2. Impact of Cryptocurrencies on Monetary Policy
   - Challenge to Monetary Control: Analysis of how cryptocurrencies, as decentralized currencies, challenge traditional monetary control exercised by central banks.
   - Influence on Exchange Rates and Inflation: Exploring the potential impact of cryptocurrencies on exchange rates and inflation rates.

3. Responses from Central Banks
   - Central Bank Digital Currencies (CBDC): Discussion on the development of CBDCs as a response from central banks to

the emergence of cryptocurrencies.
- Regulation and Surveillance: Analysis of regulatory and surveillance measures put in place by central banks to regulate the use of cryptocurrencies.

4. Cryptocurrencies and Financial Stability
- Risks to Financial Stability: Examination of the risks that cryptocurrencies may pose to financial stability, including volatility and speculative bubbles.
- Integration into the Financial System: Discussion of the challenges and opportunities related to the integration of cryptocurrencies into the global financial system.

5. Challenges and Opportunities for Central Banks
- Adaptation to Technological Innovations: Analysis of the need for central banks to adapt to technological innovations brought by cryptocurrencies.
- Currency Diversification Opportunities: Exploring opportunities for central banks to use cryptocurrencies for monetary diversification and risk reduction.

6. Future Perspectives and Developments
- Evolution of Monetary Policy in the Age of Cryptocurrencies: Reflections on the future evolution of monetary policy in the era of cryptocurrencies.
- International Collaboration and Standards: Discussion on the importance of international collaboration and establishing standards to manage the impact of cryptocurrencies on monetary policy.

Conclusion

Cryptocurrencies pose a significant challenge to traditional monetary policy, forcing central banks and regulators to rethink their approaches. As the financial landscape continues to evolve with the adoption of cryptocurrencies, central banks must find ways to integrate these new technologies while preserving financial stability. This chapter highlights the importance of a proactive and adaptive approach to addressing the challenges posed by cryptocurrencies in the area of monetary policy.

CHAPTER 37: PSYCHOLOGICAL AND BEHAVIORAL ASPECTS OF CRYPTOCURRENCIES

Introduction

Investing and trading cryptocurrencies are not just financial activities; they also encompass significant psychological and behavioral aspects. This chapter explores the psychological and behavioral dynamics that influence the decisions of investors and users of cryptocurrencies.

1. Psychology of Investing in Cryptocurrencies
  - Investor Behavior: Introduction to typical cryptocurrency investor behaviors, including cognitive and emotional biases.
  - Motivational Factors: Analysis of the motivations behind investing in cryptocurrencies, such as the search for quick wins, fear of missing out (FOMO), and belief in the technology.

2. Impact of Volatility on Behavior
  - Reactions to Market Volatility: Discussion of how volatility in cryptocurrency markets affects investor behavior, often exacerbating emotional reactions.
  - Stress and Anxiety Management: Exploring strategies to

manage stress and anxiety related to cryptocurrency price fluctuations.

3. Cognitive Bias and Decision Making
   - Identifying Cognitive Bias: Examining common cognitive biases in cryptocurrency investing, such as confirmation bias and overconfidence.
   - Strategies to Counter Bias: Discussion of strategies to recognize and counter cognitive biases in investment decision making.

4. Group Phenomena and Social Dynamics
   - Group Effect and Social Pressure: Analysis of the impact of group dynamics and social pressure on investment decisions in cryptocurrencies.
   - Role of Social Media and Online Forums: Exploring the influence of social media and online forums on investor perceptions and behaviors.

5. Financial Education and Risk Awareness
   - Importance of Financial Education: Discussion on the importance of financial education to understand the risks and realities of the cryptocurrency market.
   - Developing a Rational Approach: Tips for developing a more rational and informed approach to investing in cryptocurrencies.

6. Future Perspectives and Research
   - Future Investor Behavior Studies: Reflections on future research needs to better understand cryptocurrency investor behavior.
   - Adapting to Market Developments: Exploring how investors can adapt to future developments in the cryptocurrency market.

Conclusion

Psychological and behavioral aspects play a crucial role in investing and trading cryptocurrencies. Understanding these dynamics is essential to making informed decisions and effectively managing risks. This chapter highlights the importance of financial education, self-awareness, and emotional management in navigating the complex and often volatile world of cryptocurrencies.

CHAPTER 38: CRYPTOCURRENCIES AND INSURANCE

Introduction

The integration of cryptocurrencies in the insurance sector opens up new perspectives for risk management, underwriting and payments. This chapter explores the implications of cryptocurrencies for the insurance industry, examining how they can transform traditional operations and introduce new business models.

1. Cryptocurrencies in the Payment of Insurance Premiums
   - Payment Facilitation: Discussion on the use of cryptocurrencies to simplify and accelerate the process of paying insurance premiums.
   - Benefits for International Policyholders: Analysis of the benefits of cryptocurrency payments for international customers, eliminating transaction fees and exchange rates.
2. Cryptocurrencies and Compensation
   - Speed of Claims: Exploring the use of cryptocurrencies to speed up the claims process, providing fast and secure payments to policyholders.
   - Transparency and Fraud Reduction: Discussion of how cryptocurrencies can increase transparency and reduce the risk of compensation fraud.
3. Blockchain and Insurance Underwriting
   - Underwriting Improvement: Analysis of the impact of blockchain, the underlying technology of cryptocurrencies,

on insurance underwriting, particularly in terms of data management and risk assessment.
- Smart Contracts for Insurance Policies: Exploring the use of smart contracts to automate insurance policy execution and claims management.

4. Cryptocurrencies and Reinsurance
- Reinsurance Transaction Facilitation: Discussion on the use of cryptocurrencies to simplify and secure reinsurance transactions between companies.
- Innovation in Reinsurance Models: Analysis of the new opportunities that cryptocurrencies and blockchain offer for innovation in reinsurance models.

5. Regulatory and Compliance Challenges
- Regulatory Issues: Examination of regulatory challenges related to the acceptance of cryptocurrencies in the insurance industry, including compliance and financial regulation issues.
- Volatility Risk Management: Discussion on managing the risks associated with the volatility of cryptocurrencies in the context of insurance.

6. Future Perspectives and Innovations
- Changing Insurance Landscape: Thoughts on the potential long-term impact of cryptocurrencies on the insurance landscape.
- Cross-Sector Innovations and Collaborations: Exploring future innovations and collaboration opportunities between the insurance and fintech sectors.

Conclusion

The integration of cryptocurrencies into the insurance industry presents significant opportunities to modernize payment processes, improve risk management and introduce new business models. However, this integration must be approached with caution, taking into account regulatory challenges and market volatility. This chapter highlights the importance of a balanced and innovative approach to exploit the potential of cryptocurrencies in the insurance sector.

CHAPTER 39: CRYPTOCURRENCIES AND SOCIO-CULTURAL CHANGES

Introduction

The rise of cryptocurrencies is not limited to an economic or technological phenomenon; it also generates significant socio-cultural changes. This chapter explores the impact of cryptocurrencies on social norms, cultural behaviors and societal structures.

1. Changing Perceptions of Money
   - Evolution of Value: Discussion of how cryptocurrencies are reshaping traditional perceptions of value and money.
   - Trust and Decentralization: Analysis of the evolution of consumer trust from centralized institutions to decentralized systems.

2. Cryptocurrencies and Social Inclusion
   - Expanded Access to Financial Services: Exploring the impact of cryptocurrencies on financial inclusion, particularly for unbanked populations.
   - Reducing Economic Inequalities: Discussion on the potential of cryptocurrencies to reduce economic inequalities by providing equal access to financial resources.

3. Impact on Consumer Behavior
   - Changing Consumption Habits: Analysis of the impact of cryptocurrencies on consumption habits, including online

purchases and money transfers.
- Adoption of Blockchain Technologies: Exploring how the adoption of blockchain technologies influences consumer behaviors and expectations for transparency and security.

4. Cryptocurrencies and Youth Culture
- Engagement of Younger Generations: Discussion on the appeal of cryptocurrencies for younger generations and their impact on youth culture, particularly in terms of investment and innovation.
- Education and Awareness: Analysis of the importance of education and awareness about cryptocurrencies for younger generations.

5. Ethical and Social Challenges
- Ethical Issues and Responsibility: Examination of the ethical issues raised by the use of cryptocurrencies, including corporate social responsibility in this area.
- Impact on Social Relations and Work: Discussion of the impact of cryptocurrencies on social relations and work structures, including self-employment and decentralized economies.

6. Future Perspectives and Cultural Adaptation
- Evolution of Social and Cultural Norms: Reflections on the future evolution of social and cultural norms under the influence of cryptocurrencies.
- Adaptation of Institutions and Policies: Exploring the need for institutions and policies to adapt to the emergence of cryptocurrencies and their societal impact.

Conclusion

Cryptocurrencies are not just an economic phenomenon; they also represent a driver of socio-cultural change. By changing perceptions of value, influencing consumer behavior and reshaping social structures, cryptocurrencies are redefining many aspects of contemporary society. This chapter highlights the importance of understanding and embracing these changes, while addressing the ethical and social challenges they present.

CHAPTER 40: INTERACTIONS BETWEEN CRYPTOCURRENCIES AND OTHER EMERGING TECHNOLOGIES

Introduction

The intersection of cryptocurrencies with other emerging technologies creates a landscape rich in innovation and possibility. This chapter explores how cryptocurrencies interact with technologies such as artificial intelligence (AI), Internet of Things (IoT), augmented reality (AR) and virtual reality (VR), shaping new applications and transforming various sectors.

1. Cryptocurrencies and Artificial Intelligence
   - Trading Optimization and Forecasting: Analysis of the use of AI to optimize cryptocurrency trading strategies and predict market trends.
   - Security and Risk Management: Discussion on the application of AI in fraud detection and risk management in cryptocurrency transactions.
2. Cryptocurrencies and the Internet of Things (IoT)

- **Automated Transactions in IoT:** Exploring the use of cryptocurrencies to facilitate automatic and secure transactions between IoT devices.
- **IoT-Based Business Models:** Analysis of innovative business models emerging at the intersection of IoT and cryptocurrencies, such as micropayments systems for IoT services.

3. Cryptocurrencies, Augmented Reality and Virtual Reality
   - **Immersive Trading Experiences:** Discussion on using AR and VR to create immersive and interactive cryptocurrency trading experiences.
   - **Virtual Currencies in Virtual Worlds:** Exploring the integration of cryptocurrencies into virtual worlds and metaverse platforms, facilitating transactions and digital ownership.

4. Blockchain, Cryptocurrencies and Big Data
   - **Data Analytics for Cryptocurrency Markets:** Analyzing the use of Big Data to gain insights into cryptocurrency markets and improve investment decisions.
   - **Data Security and Transparency:** Discussion on the contribution of blockchain to the security and transparency of massive data.

5. Challenges and Limitations
   - **Technical Complexity and Integration:** Examines the technical challenges of integrating cryptocurrencies with other emerging technologies.
   - **Regulatory and Compliance Issues:** Analysis of the regulatory and compliance issues that arise at the intersection of these technologies.

6. Future Perspectives and Innovations
   - **Transversal Technological Innovations:** Reflections on future innovations that could emerge from the convergence of these technologies with cryptocurrencies.
   - **Impact on Industries and Society:** Exploring the potential impact of these technological interactions on various industries and on society as a whole.

Conclusion
The interaction of cryptocurrencies with other emerging technologies opens up scope for innovation and transformation in many sectors. From optimizing trading to creating new user experiences in virtual worlds, these technological convergences promise to reshape the way we see and interact with the financial world and beyond. This chapter highlights the importance of navigating this evolving landscape with a thorough understanding and strategic approach to fully exploit the potential of these interconnected technologies.

www.ingramcontent.com/pod-product-compliance
Lightning Source LLC
Chambersburg PA
CBHW071100240526
45471CB00016B/2173